Edgar Cayce's Sphinx, The Hall of Records & The Holy Grail

John Bunker
Karen Pressler

Edgar Cayce's Sphinx, the Hall of Records & the Holy Grail

Copyright ©2020 by John M. Bunker & Karen L. Pressler

Bunker Pressler Books

"Two and a Guide"

Back cover image taken from a 3000 year-old vignette from the Djedkhonsuiefankh funerary papyrus on display in the Cairo Egyptian Museum.

Questions regarding this book can be addressed to:

Bunker Pressler Books
8829 Heffelfinger Rd.
Churubusco, IN 46723

Bunker.Pressler@gmail.com
https://sites.google.com/site/edgarcayceandthehallofrecords/

Table of Contents

PREFACE 1
THE HISTORY OF THE HALL OF RECORDS 3
THE HISTORY OF THE SPHINX 11
BIBLIOGRAPHY 27

PREFACE

In 1932, one of the compilers of Edgar Cayce's *Search for God* lessons heard a voice say, "It is time for you to take the Holy Grail." When Cayce was asked about this while he was in a state of self-hypnosis, he replied,

> *"The reading of the quest of the Holy Grail at the present time would bring to the body the proper interpretation of how and what the vision should mean."* [1]

Someone once said the Hall of Records has become every Egyptologist's Holy Grail.[2] Oddly enough the Hall of Records, like the Holy Grail, has not yet been found. It is said to be located in an area of land that measures less than one square mile and the search for it has been ongoing for nearly a century. Edgar Cayce gave the position of the Hall of Records in many of his psychic readings, with many different points of reference, on many different occasions. But no matter how Cayce described the location of the Hall of Records, his directions were misunderstood. While it is true that the style of grammar in the Cayce readings is notoriously difficult to understand at first glance, it isn't an obstacle if enough effort is made to become familiar with it. For more insight into the language of the Cayce readings, refer to the article written by Gina Cerminara, "The Language of the Edgar Cayce Readings." Her article of December 1945 was reprinted in the April 1966 A.R.E. Journal available from Edgar Cayce's A.R.E., The Association for Research and Enlightenment.

---

[1] Edgat Cayce Reading 262-34, paragraph 7.
[2] Whiteman, Y. (2018, March 18). The Kolbrin: On Who Built The Great Sphinx, And Why. Graham Hancock Official Website. https://grahamhancock.com/whitemany6/

Scene from *Indiana Jones and the Raiders of the Lost Ark*

THE HISTORY OF THE HALL OF RECORDS

It has long been believed that the Hall of Records is located between the paws of the Sphinx, but did Cayce ever specify that? Or did he use the Sphinx as a survey marker to indicate the direction of the position of the Hall of Records? In surveying, a straight line is needed, and to create a straight line two points are needed, so to illustrate this Cayce used the Sphinx and the position of an observer, and the shadow cast by that observer (see p. 18). When the sun arose in the sky and the line of the shadow of the observer fell between the paws of the Sphinx, it created an alignment with the position of the Hall of Records beyond the Sphinx.[3]

So we decided to write this brief history of the Hall of Records with the hope it may be more clearly understood. We have included many footnotes in this booklet for reference and verification. (To those who actually take time to read and verify footnotes, we applaud you.)

According to the Cayce readings, the history of the Hall of Records begins with Atlantis. More than a quarter of a million years ago[4] upheavals in the land prompted some of the populace to leave by ship.[5]

---

[3] Edgar Cayce Reading 2402-2, paragraph 38.
[4] Edgar Cayce Reading 341-9, paragraph 4
[5] Edgar Cayce Reading 993-3, paragraph 15: *during upheaval sojourn*; and 813-1, paragraph 24: *when the upheavals began that made of the egress of many from that city of the Poseidon land*; 5748-6, paragraph 17: *In those periods when the first change had come in the position of the land, there had been an egress of peoples – or THINGS – from the Atlantean land, when the Nile (of Nole then) emptied into what is now the Atlantic Ocean, on the Congo end of the country;*

4

Mouth of the Nile previous to the formation of the Delta, when the Mediterranean Ocean reached to the foot of the sandy plateau on which the Pyramids stand.

342-8, paragraph 17: *the monuments of the THINGS afterwards became a stumbling block.*

[6] Maspero, *The Dawn of Civilization*, 1922, page 5

Their journey took them across the ocean to the Bay of Biscay and the Pyrenees Mountains[7] and then to the Mediterranean Ocean, which reached to the foot of the sandy plateau on which the Pyramids stand.[8]   Then the land of Egypt was known as the land of Nole.[9]

Today the Nile flows north into the Mediterranean as the result of the collision of tectonic plates that began in the remote past, which uplifted the surface of the earth to create a continental divide. But before that, in ancient times, the Nile River did not empty into the Mediterranean Sea. Instead, it flowed south into the Atlantic on the Congo end of the country. The surface of the continent was different then and the Sahara Desert was a fertile land.[10] The facing image shows the mouth of the Nile prior to the formation of the Delta, when the Mediterranean Ocean reached to the foot of the sandy plateau on which the Pyramids stand.

More than a quarter of a million years ago, refugees from Atlantis built a city at the edge of the water[11] and constructed the first of the Egyptian pyramids[12] near the Mokattam hill region, where there was a supply of coarse limestone that could be used as construction material for masonry.

---

[7] Edgar Cayce Reading 364-4, paragraph 5. "With this also came the first egress of peoples to that of the Pyrenees first, OF which later we find that peoples who enter into the black or the mixed peoples, in what later became the Egyptian dynasty."
[8] Maspero, *The Dawn of Civilization*, 1922, page 3.
[9] Edgar Cayce Reading 5748-6, paragraph 17
[10] Edgar Cayce Reading 5748-6, paragraph 17.
[11] Edgar Cayce Reading 5748-16, paragraph 17: a city was built at the edge of the land
[12] See Edgar Cayce Reading 993-1, paragraph 21, and 993-3, paragraph 15

Stone quarry beside the Khafre pyramid

But after much time had passed, geologic changes caused the land in this part of the country to become submerged undersea.[13] With the passage of time the land re-emerged and the water receded, leaving the land covered with an accumulation of the sand of seabeds.[14] This is where the story of the Hall of Records begins in the history of Egypt. Ra-Ta's[15] tribe entered into Egypt during the years of 11,016[16] through 11,013 BC[17]. With this entering in there began archaeological research[18] and the removal of mounds of sand, which covered the remains of immense structures left by the previous civilization,[19] including enormous megalithic monuments seemly intended by their creators to stand forever. Then the rebuilding began.[20]

---

[13] Edgar Cayce Reading 341-9, paragraph 4, *we find this same country had been submerged for nearly a quarter of a million years since the civilization had been in this portion of the country.*

[14] Edgar Cayce Reading 341-9, paragraph 5: *The monuments that were unearthed and added to from time to time, we find are some still existent, though many buried beneath shifting sands, others underneath sands that became the bed of the seas that overflowed this country.*; 341-8, paragraph 17: *The monuments of the THINGS afterward became a stumbling block.*

[15] Ra-Ta was a former incarnation of Edgar Cayce.

[16] Edgar Cayce Reading 341-8, paragraph 17: *indicating that this particular period in Egypt was eleven thousand and sixteen (11,016 B.C.)...a [Ra – Ta period]*

[17] Edgar Cayce Reading 341-9, paragraph 7: *This coming, as given, in the eleven thousand thirteen to sixteen (11,013 to 16) years before the Prince of Peace*

[18] Edgar Cayce Reading 6748-6.paragraph 16: *there was even then the seeking through those channels that today are called archaeological research*

[19] Edgar Cayce Reading 341-9, paragraph 5: *the monuments as were unearthed and added to from time to time, we find some are still existent, though many are buried beneath shifting sands.*

[20] Edgar Cayce Reading 5748-6, paragraph 17: *they began to build upon those mounds that were discovered through research*

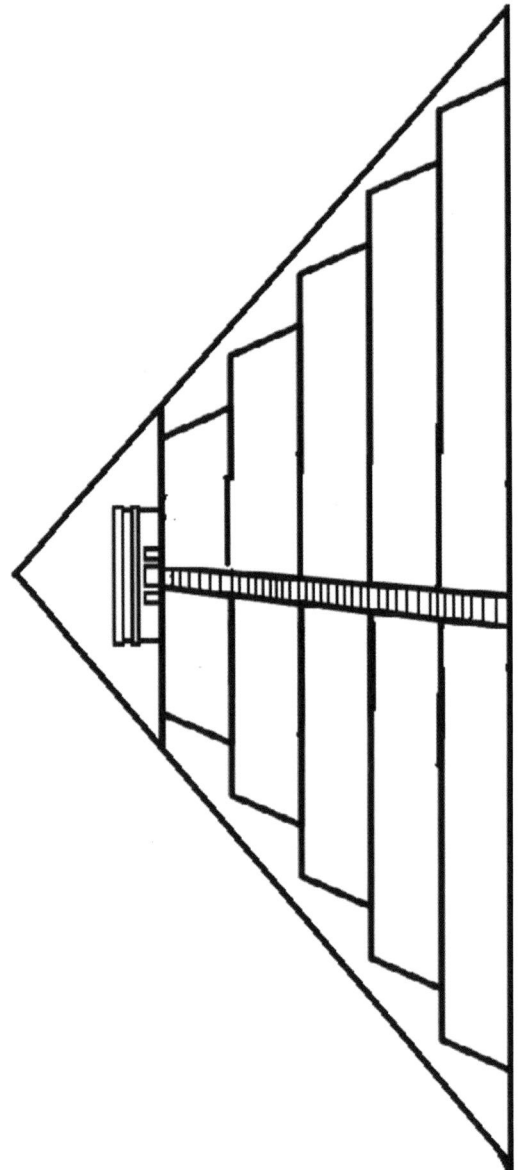

Temple of records in a pyramid of its own added to top of mound.

From time to time monuments were unearthed and added to[21] as the Kingdom of Egypt developed. After excavation at the top of one of the mounds at Giza, a temple was constructed in which was stored the history of the world from the beginning, when spirit first took shape in material form.[22] Thus was the creation of the Hall of Records in a temple or pyramid of its own,[23] on top of a more ancient mound of stone. The change in workmanship where the rebuilding began is visible even today on the pyramid now known as Khafre's.

---

[21] Edgar Cayce Reading 341-9, paragraph 5.
[22] Edgar Cayce Reading 378-16, paragraph 11.
[23] Edgar Cayce Reading 2329-3, paragraph 36.

10

This was later turned into the lion with the man.

---

[24] https://egypt-museum.com/post/619491264591806464/great-sphinx-of-giza-and-the-pyramid-of-khafre#gsc.tab=0

THE HISTORY OF THE SPHINX

Just as Mount Rushmore commemorates former presidents of the United States of America, a gigantic carving of a human head representing an important Egyptian official was created by sculpting a massive limestone rock that protruded up from the plateau, about a quarter mile east of the Hall of Records. This was to commemorate his devotion and service to Egypt. Before the Sphinx came into being, it was only the sculptured face[25] on a stone head intended to be a memorial.

---

[25] Edgar Cayce Reading 457-2, paragraph 11: *the facing of what afterward became the sphinx*

This was later turned into the lion with the man.[26] The face stood alone for more than a century before the body of a lion was created under it by excavation.

[27]

Why was the Sphinx created? It was intended to show all the people of the land the relationships of man and the animal, the beast as a part of man's consciousness, and to symbolize the changes in the creature that has become man in the earth. Thus developed the mystery of the ages; the Sphinx. [28]

---

[26] Edgar Cayce Reading 5748-6, paragraph 17: *That which is now called the Mystery of Mysteries, this was intended to be a MEMORIAL - as would be termed today - to that counsellor who ruled or governed, or who acted in the capacity of the director in the MATERIAL things in the land. With the return of the priest (as it had been stopped), this was later - by Isis, the queen, or the daughter of Ra - turned so as to present to those peoples in that land the relationships of man and the animal or carnal world with those changes that fade or fall away in their various effect. These may be seen in a different manner presented in many of the various sphinxes, as called, in other portions of the land - as the lion with the man...*

[27] http://giza.fas.harvard.edu/sites/2080/allphotos/

[28] Edgar Cayce Reading 5748-6, paragraph 17.

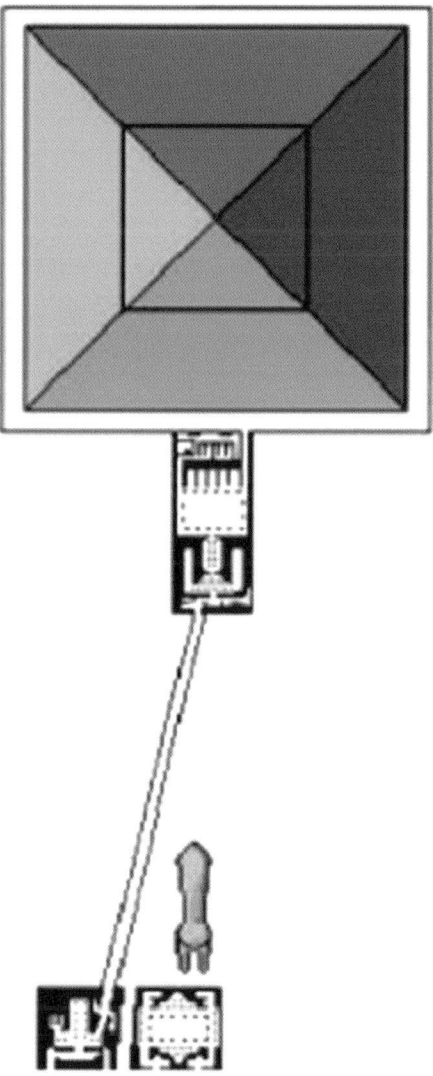

Viewed from above, these initial ancient monuments on the plateau of Giza looked like this.

The readings state there is "passage from the right paw of the Sphinx to this entrance of the record chamber." The hall of records is also described as "the chambers of the way between the Sphinx and the pyramid, in a pyramid of its own." The pyramid faces the Sphinx that was "later set as the sentinel or guard." Threaded throughout a number of readings given over a period of years, Cayce made specific comments about the location of the Hall of Records. By gathering some of these scattered details and looking at them together, we can get a better understanding of their combined meaning. Consider the following readings:

- Reading number 5748-6, 7/1/32, paragraph 17:
  "With the storehouse, or record house (where the records are still to be uncovered), there is a chamber or passage from the right forepaw to this entrance of the record chamber, or record tomb."

- Reading number 378-16, 10/29/33, paragraph 14 describes the position of the hall of records:
  "This in position lies as the sun rises from the waters, the line of shadow (or light) falls between the paws of the Sphinx that was later set as the sentinel or guard..." (see p.18)

- Reading 2329-3, 5/1/41, paragraph 36 states that that the hall of records *"lies along the entrance that leads from the Sphinx to the pyramid, in a pyramid of its own."*

- In reading 1486-1, 11/26/37, paragraph 29, more details of the location of the hall of records is imbedded within the text, *"The data yet to be found from the chambers of the way between the sphinx and the pyramid of records."*

- Reading 2012-1, 9/25/35, paragraph 31 states, *"The place that leadeth from the Sphinx to the Hall of Records in the Egyptian land."*[29]

Collectively the foregoing, fragmentary comments provide these ideas: There is passage from the right forepaw of the Sphinx to this entrance. This sealed room in position lies west of the Sphinx along the entrance that leads from the Sphinx to the pyramid.

---

[29] Edgar Cayce Reading 2012-1, paragraph 31.

Originally the pyramid was surrounded by a walled court with the entrance into the court via the causeway.

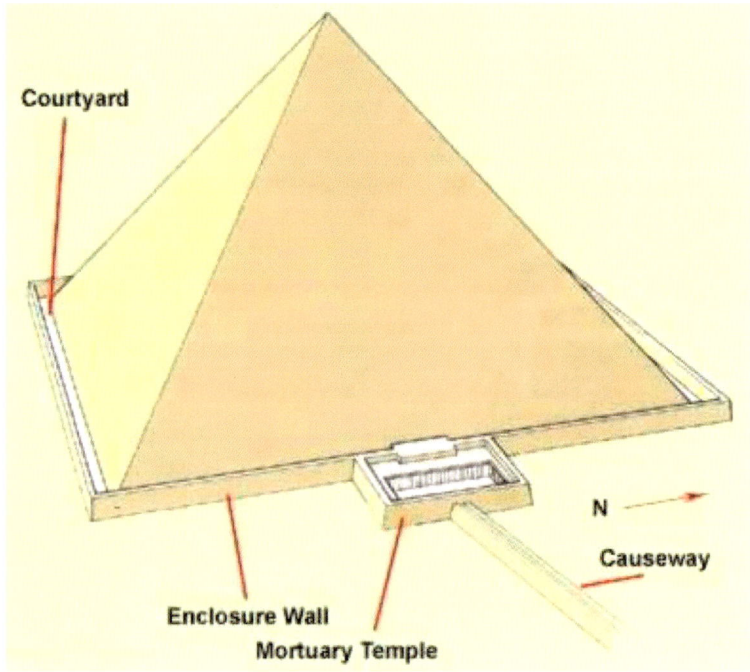

The causeway from the Sphinx to the pyramid is expressed by these four different words in these readings:

1. Passage
2. Entrance
3. Way
4. Place

The readings never used the word "tunnel" to describe the means of access to the Hall of Records, nor do they say the position of the Hall of Records is beneath the Sphinx. Considering these four synonyms, it is unlikely that the readings intended to convey the idea that there is an underground tunnel.

In this illustration the causeway is a way of passage from the right paw of the Sphinx to the pyramid.

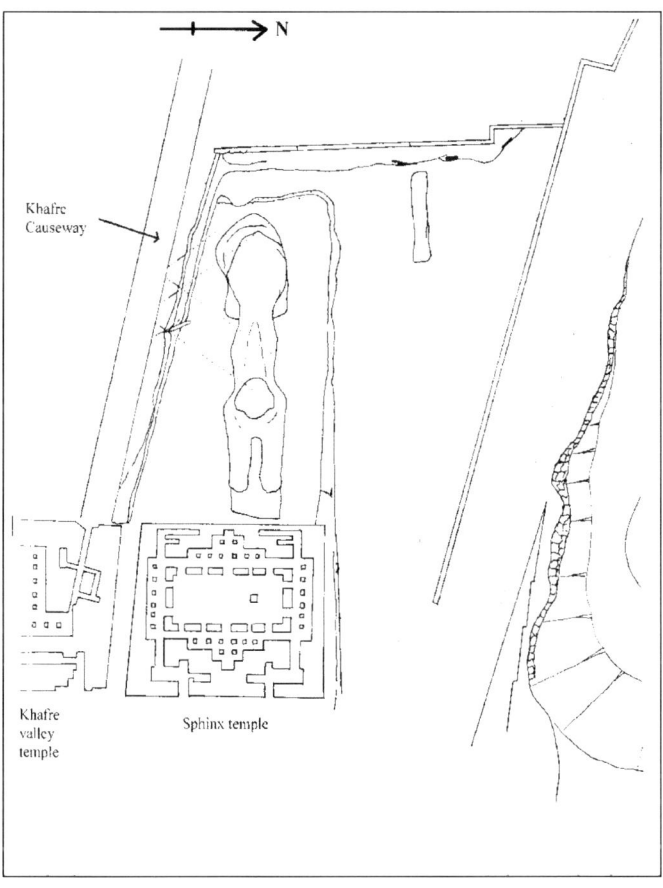

"Between then the Sphinx and the river." These words were intended to refer to the position of the observer

In an attempt to explain and clarify the location of the sealed room of the hall of records, reading 378-16, paragraph 11 states:

> "This in position lies, as the sun rises from the waters, the line of the shadow (or light) falls between the paws of the Sphinx, that was later set as the sentinel or guard, and which may not be entered from the connecting chambers from the Sphinx's paw (right paw) until the TIME has been fulfilled when the changes must be active in this sphere of man's experience. Between, then, the Sphinx and the river."

The facing illustration will aid in visualizing the intended meaning of the above reading.

What it means is this: If an observer were standing east of the Sphinx at dawn, the active change of the sun rising up from below the horizon would create a shadow of the observer that would fall toward the Sphinx, making an alignment with the observer and the Sphinx, toward the position of the chamber of records, located in the pyramid beyond the Sphinx. Now it can be understood what Cayce meant when he said, "Between then the Sphinx and the river." These words were intended to refer to the position of the observer whose shadow was cast between the paws of the Sphinx.

The causeway from the right forepaw of the Sphinx leads to the pyramid of records that contains the sealed room of records, which may be reached through the chambers that are connected to it.

20

This photograph of the Gizeh Plateau was taken in 1934. The causeway from the Sphinx to the pyramid had not yet been excavated.[30]

---

[30] This 1934 photo is courtesy of the Martin and Osa Johnson Safari Museum and is used with permission.

But what did Cayce mean when he said, *"until the TIME has been fulfilled when the changes must be active in this sphere of man's experience?"*

- This sphere of man's experience is this sphere we call Earth.

When would the time be fulfilled?

- Changes in the position of the sun and shadows are the active changes that happen as the sun rises in the sky. The length of shadows changes as the sun rises higher and higher. When the sun's position is high enough, it will cast a shadow of an observer (whom is standing between the Sphinx and the river) toward the Sphinx between its paws, thus creating an alignment with the position of the pyramid that houses the sealed room of records.

In 1932[31] Edgar Cayce described the causeway as "the way between the Sphinx and the Pyramid".[32] This causeway was not uncovered until 1936, four years after Cayce identified it. It provides a way of *passage from the right forepaw* to the pyramid.[33]

During the many years of research into the location of the Hall of Records, from time to time we exchanged ideas with Edgar Evans Cayce about it. On one of these occasions, he brought up a phrase he remembered from the readings, *"between the Sphinx and the Nile,"* which he had always thought

---

[31] Edgar Cayce Reading 5748-16, paragraph 17.
[32] Edgar Cayce Reading 1486-1, paragraph 29.
[33] Edgar Cayce Reading 5748-6, paragraph 17.

22

The Sphinx was between this storehouse and the Nile.

referred to the Hall of Records, reading 993-3, given on 10/21/31:

> "...*for the later pyramids, or those yet not uncovered, that has been spoken of, are BETWEEN the Sphinx (or the Mystery) AND the Nile, or the river...*"

We found clarification in reading 2124-3, paragraph 15, given on 10/2/31:

> *(Q) In referring to the uncovered pyramids in the Egyptian land, near what present place are these pyramids?*
> *(A) Between that as is known as the Mystery of the Ages and the river*

We came to the conclusion that this statement was talking about pyramids that were built later than the pyramid of the Hall of Records, and it was these later pyramids that were between the Sphinx and the river Nile. These are probably now located somewhere under the city of Cairo.

Another reading that has caused some confusion is reading 5748-005, paragraph 2. The grammar is somewhat difficult to follow:

> "*There was first that attempt to restore and to add to that which had been begun on what is called the Sphinx, and the treasure or storehouse facing same, between this and the Nile.*"

Is this reading referring to the Sphinx or to the storehouse with these words: *between this and the Nile?*[34]

---

[34] Edgar Cayce Reading 5748 5, paragraph 2. EC: *Yes. In the information as respecting the pyramids, their purpose in the experience of the peoples, in the period when there was the rebuilding of the priest during the return in the land, some 10,500 before the coming of the Christ into the land, there was first that attempt to restore and to add to that which had been begun on what is called the Sphinx, and the treasure or storehouse facing same, between this and the Nile, in which those records were kept by Arart and Araaraart in the period.*

This reading was an attempt to show the position of the memorial that later became the Sphinx, using two geographic locations for reference: the first was the storehouse, the second was the Nile.

When will the Hall of Records be opened? This might be answered by reading 2329-3, paragraphs 39-40:

> 39. (Q) How may I now find those records, or should I wait — or must I wait?
>
> (A) You will find the records by that channel as indicated, as these may be obtained MENTALLY. As for the physical records, - it will be necessary to wait until the full time has come for the breaking up of much that has been in the nature of selfish motives in the world. For, remember, these records were made from the angle of WORLD movements. So must thy activities be in the present of the universal approach, but as applied to the individual. Keep the faith. Know that the ability lies within self. As ye were then the offspring of, and the helpmeet to, that one who bore such an influence upon the movements of mankind through that period, so may thy power, thy might, thy love, thy faith, thy abilities do much for mankind in these dark hours again. Hold fast to the faith of thy fathers.
>
> 40. We are through for the present.

The beginning of a new era is upon us. What will it become? As the future is unveiled before us, let us visualize the Forces of Harmony, Peace, Love and Understanding at work in this sphere of man's development. Let us see in our fellows that which we worship in our Creator. There is no better time to begin than now.

Seek to awaken your inner self. Seek the knowledge of the light that burns ever within you.

Let each of us be a channel of blessings to others.

FINIS

BIBLIOGRAPHY

Cayce, E. (1993). *The complete Edgar Cayce readings*. Virginia Beach, Va.: A.R.E. Press.

Cerminara, Gina. "The Language of the Edgar Cayce Readings," *A.R.E. Bulletin (*Dec. 1945*)*; reprinted in *The A.R.E. Journal* (Apr. 1966*)*, Association for Research and Enlightenment, Virginia Beach, Va.

Maspero, G., Sayce, A. H., & McClure, M. L. (1922). *The dawn of civilization: Egypt and Chaldea*. London: Society for Promoting Christian Knowledge.

Whiteman, Y. (2018, March 18). "The Kolbrin: On Who Built the Great Sphinx, and Why." Graham Hancock Official Website. https://grahamhancock.com/whitemany6/

ABOUT THE AUTHORS

John Bunker and Karen Pressler have been researching and writing together since 1993, when they discovered the Edgar Cayce readings and began to study the history of mankind from the remote past, and the lost knowledge from those earliest times. The research has included the study of hieroglyphics, Egyptology, and Astronomy, and their books can be found on Amazon.

Today their home is in rural Indiana where they live in harmony with nature and enjoy boating, gardening, family, and their feline friends.

Printed in Great Britain
by Amazon